The Gift of the Snowflake

Jackie Hirschi

ISBN 979-8-88851-400-9 (Paperback)
ISBN 979-8-88851-401-6 (Digital)

Covenant Books
11661 Hwy 707
Murrells Inlet, SC 29576
www.covenantbooks.com

Victoria lay in her bed, gently running her fingers through the natural ash-blond locks of her granddaughter's hair. As Olivia lay asleep at her side, Victoria marveled at Olivia's curls and the way they surrounded her angelic face. These locks of gold only enhanced Olivia's innocence. As they lay together, huddled in Victoria's warm bed, Victoria pondered as to the wisdom which Olivia possessed, having left her pre-mortal existence only four years prior. Victoria always believed that this precious knowledge was never wiped completely from one's mind but faded gradually over time.

Victoria had been given proof of this belief as Olivia had included in her conversations with Victoria comments concerning Heavenly Father and eternal concepts, which she was far too young to have ever understood. Yet Olivia spoke as if she had retained full memory of the wonderment and joy she had previously known. When Victoria questioned Olivia as to where she had acquired this knowledge, Olivia only shrugged her small shoulders and said, "I don't know. I just know it." Yes, she just knew it. She knew and understood the workings of our Heavenly Father far more than many men or women who had spent a lifetime searching.

As they lay together, Olivia engulfed in Victoria's arms, Victoria contemplated the wonders Olivia could have shared with her as she held her in her arms less than fifteen minutes after her physical body had taken its first mortal breath. Victoria recognized Olivia immediately, and as Olivia opened her eyes wide for the first time and stared without hesitation at Victoria, it was evident that Olivia also, despite the lack of focus offered by her new earth eyes, recognized Victoria. Finally, they were together again even though their spirits were never truly apart.

These two souls had known each other before this world began. The force that surrounds this grandmother and grand-daughter is a power beyond any that existed in this mortal realm. No amount of separation could ever allow either of them to have forgotten the other. They were meant to be together. They were eternally and now earthly linked, and as Olivia grew, the connection between the two grew deeper. How blessed Victoria was to have all of her granddaughters, and how blessed they all were to have Victoria.

Victoria drew Olivia closer to her chest. She could now feel Olivia's warm breath on her neck. At this stage in her young life, Olivia was unable to comprehend the love which Victoria deeply possessed for her. Victoria often informed Olivia that she would fight dragons for her. This was a devotion that Olivia understood, for she, like many other little girls, enjoyed the fanciful fairytales that included dragons and the belief that every-one lived happily ever after. But was there truly a happily ever after? Was this notion as wonderful as it seemed? This perfect child of God who lay in Victoria's arms will be forced to face enormous evils that lay in wait to destroy her perfect spirit. For this purpose, Victoria was prepared to fight dragons, evil dragons. It was her job. Being a grandmother did not make her any less accountable for raising, teaching, and protecting her granddaughters.

Victoria had been promised in a blessing many years prior that she would always be surrounded by children. Now that this promise had come to pass, she delighted in the seven delicate and perfect princesses who called her grandma. "Grandma," Victoria whispered quietly to herself, what a perfect calling. It is far better than a mother, wife, sister, or daughter. Now in the midst of all of the pink and bows that filled Victoria's life, she had been awarded a mini version of herself, Oliva. This small human possessed a great number of qualities in personality and looks that forced everyone to acknowledge without reservation that Victoria was her grandmother.

As the cold December air began to penetrate the window above the bed, Victoria reached for the additional blanket that lay folded nicely at her feet. As she pulled it over the two of them, Victoria reflected on how she had always loved the feel of this particular blanket's soft velvety fabric. Victoria had received the blanket as a Christmas gift ten years prior from her mother. Despite the lumps that had gathered in the batting and the many repairs that could be witnessed along the edging, the blanket remained Victoria's favorite. It brought her comfort each time she wraps it around her body. She often imagined her mother's arms surrounding her, loving her, and protecting her. Despite Victoria's age, there was still a need, a satisfaction in her knowing how much her mother still loved her just as she had when she was a child.

Victoria was soon lost in the memories of her childhood. Many of them were not happy, yet she always saw the many sacrifices her mother made, especially at Christmas. Even in times of financial hardship, there were always gifts under the tree. These memories were so precious and magical as the number of joyous memories that Victoria possessed was greatly limited.

Victoria was raised in an extremely unstable home. The anger her father inflicted upon the family was done so by physical and mental means. Victoria remembered the yelling, pain, and fear that she was forced to endure in her own personal encounters with her father. Not only did she maintain visions of her own abuse, but also that which was inflicted upon her mother. Every child who witnesses the brutal treatment of their mother experiences a lifetime of guilt, being unable to stop the violence.

These memories quickly broke Victoria's peace. She had worked for decades to remove such thoughts from her mind, yet they were forever burned into her soul. Yet as a child, Christmas seemed to bring with it a small sense of peace. This was a block of time in which her father seemed to possess the ability to dismiss his hateful acts. It was almost a peace, a reprieve from the evil that rested over her home. It may have been for a day or as little as an afternoon, but Victoria was grateful for that brief moment. Victoria came to see it as the eye of the hurricane, where a calm lay even as the areas on which it stood had been destroyed and the winds and sea circled violently around them. There, in that eye, the sun shone. The air was pure, and gratitude for that brief moment was praised. For this, despite the negative stigma that had been placed on most of the events in her life, Christmas had remained Victoria's favorite. No force of nature including that of man could ever take the joy that Christmas presented her away. She would not allow it. She protected it, reverently guarded it as if a sacred shrine.

Because of the sacred relevance of the Christmas season, Victoria was determined to not allow it to be swept up in the legend of Santa Clause. As much as she loved the tale of the jolly old elf, she wanted more; she wanted her family to have more. She loved each one of them so deeply that she refused to allow her home to be consumed by the possessions of the world. Worldly gifts, as wonderful as they were to give and receive, often disappeared as quickly as they came, but the gift of the Savior was eternal.

As the warmth of the blankets cradled Victoria, her thoughts quickly focused on Mary, the mother of the Savior of the world. How deep was the mortal and eternal bond that existed between Mary and her Son Jesus? Yes, he was the Savior of the world. Yes, he had a preordained purpose. Yes, she knew that his life was not to mirror that of other sons, but he was the blood of her blood, the flesh of her flesh. Mary was always going to be a part of the Savior's life while on the earth and beyond, a mother and son's undying bond.

Victoria knew of that bond. She knew the joy a child brings into one's life. She could also testify to the pain that a mother experiences when her child is hurt or in despair. Mary knew that pain. She knew the pain of a mother as they witness their child being mocked, rejected, and harmed. She knew the pain of seeing the anguish and torture in her child's eyes. And then the final thrust of the knife, the dagger to one's heart, the loss, physical loss.

In her mind's eye, Victoria visioned Mary kneeling before the Savior, before her Son, as he hung above her upon the cross. The image was mesmerizing as she, for a brief moment of time, could feel the pain of one mother to another. The reality of the experience quickly shook Victoria's mind back to reality. *How could Mary have ever endured such agony? I cannot believe that the knowledge of her son fulfilling God's plan protected her from the pain. She loved him so. He was hers. He was given to her to care for, raise, and protect. She brought him into this world. now she had to witness him taken violently from it for no reason other than who he was, the Son of God.*

As Victoria lay motionless, tears fell upon her cheeks and then rolled gently upon Olivia's forehead. Only Mary will ever know the blessing and the sorrow she experienced on the day her Son was born. Only Mary will ever know the joy of raising him, loving him, and of the lessons that, through his mission on earth, personally taught her. As Joseph stood at Mary's side and experienced for himself this gift of the Savior's birth to the world, it was Mary, his mother, who experienced the glory of heaven at its greatest moment.

Victoria gave Olivia a tight squeeze, causing her to awaken briefly and then drift back into her winter slumber. No longer did Victoria possess the ability to sleep, which is something she had hoped would absorb her before the clock struck midnight. The last time Victoria had glanced at the dimly lit clock beside her bed, it was 11:21 p.m. Now as she peered at it once again, it read 11:56 p.m. Soon, it would be December 2. Only four minutes separated Victoria from the one-year anniversary of her breakdown. A breakdown that released a great amount of pain that had built up inside her for over forty-five years, but in doing so, it brought pain and disappointment to her husband and children.

Victoria had always lived to satisfy the needs and desires of others. As a child, she was taught to do all within her power to not upset her father, to walk on eggshells, and to cater to his needs. As she became a wife and mother, she continued to act in a similar manner. Never did she think of herself but lived only for those she cared for. Now as Victoria's children had grown into adults, she still worried and did all within her power to care for them, to aid them whenever possible. That is what a mother does, yet her children were not happy with her. Victoria became overwhelmed with the confusion and frustration she experienced in regard to their actions and comments.

She did not interfere in the lives of her married children. Her life now focused only on her grandchildren, yet for the first time in her life, she saw herself as an unfit parent. The actions of her children and husband led her to believe that she was correct in her assumption. Now one year after her breakdown, some of her children harbored a sense of anger toward their mother after witnessing her emotionally and physically crumble before them. The anger they possessed had not vanished; maybe it never would.

"I am me. I want to be no one but who I am," Victoria whispered. The spontaneity of her personality had always left her open to judgment and ridicule by others. Her artistic nature caused her to view her surroundings differently. As individuals look at things for what they are, Victoria always saw them for what they could be. Instead of relying on instructions, patterns, or blueprints to accomplish a task, Victoria examined an item and, in her mind, could determine its assembly and replicate or resolve an item or issue.

Victoria never fit into the family in which she was born. The difference in her personality compared to that of her parents and siblings labeled her as a troublemaker. She had always wanted to believe that she was special, of value, and possessed the riches that life had to offer. But the control both her parents demanded over their children placed great limits on Victoria and her creativity.

Victoria had been happily married to Kurt now for thirty-five years. When she married Kurt, he possessed custody of his daughter Chelsie from a previous marriage. Chelsie was eight at the time of their marriage, and as they built their family, Chelsie fit right in. Yet over time, as Chelsie began to display resistance to having Victoria as a mother figure, Victoria was determined to make it work. Yet as Chelsie grew, she made decisions that were not in her best interest. Chelsie often did so as a means of gaining the attention of her father, which she had now been forced to share with four other siblings.

Chelsie married right out of high school and months later, gave birth to the first of five children. During these years, Chelsie always questioned the lost bond between her and her own biological mother and found more and more fault with Victoria, hindering family relationships. In time, Chelsie separated herself from Victoria and Kurt. Attempts to reunite the family failed as hurt built on both sides. It was time to let Chelsie and her family go. Yet as Chelsie wished for separation from Kurt and Victoria, she continued to remain connected with her siblings as well as Victoria's parents.

Victoria was now surrounded by a husband, children, in-laws, and grandchildren. She was happy, at least on the surface. Her family was in no way perfect, yet no family is. If one was to examine the smiles on the faces found in a family portrait, one would begin to wonder what was going on behind those smiles. What have they hidden from the world?

Life is messy. It is hard. It is a journey that leads us down the roads of sunshine, and then, without warning, we are traveling down a dark, rocky path alone, with the feeling of fear overwhelming us. We begin to doubt our beliefs and, most of all, the support of those we believed loved us.

These thoughts were the toxic memories Victoria did not want to become engaged in, especially tonight of all nights. She lay looking at the patterns which the nightlight made across the wall of her bedroom. She closed her eyes and quietly said, "Please, Heavenly Father, allow me to rest, allow my mind to be at peace." Yes, peace. "Peace on Earth, goodwill toward men" (Luke 2:14 KJV).

How brilliantly those words rang out in Victoria's mind! "Good will, good will toward men," Victoria repeated softly as she buried her lips in the lush locks of Olivia's hair and kissed her head. Olivia's lavender-scented locks delighted Victoria as she thought back on the bubble bath that they had taken together just a few hours earlier. "This is my peace, my peace on earth," said Victoria.

Olivia began to move and stretched her arms high over her head. Her eyes opened wide, and a smile came over her lips. "Is it Christmas yet?" Olivia said in a sleepy voice.

"Not yet, my sweeties. Go back to sleep." Olivia kissed Victoria's hand which rested against her cheek and fell back to sleep.

Unable to sleep, Victoria gently climbed out of bed so as to not disturb Olivia. Tomorrow was going to be filled with holiday festivities; she would need her rest. Victoria looked forward to creating holiday traditions with her granddaughters. Last year, she was not able to spend time with them to decorate cookies, read stories, ride a sleigh, and, of course, decorate a larger-than-life gingerbread house, one that could only be made by Victoria.

Victoria arose and sat on the edge of her bed. She shook her head at the pile of clothes that lay in front of the closet. Kurt had never been able to get his clothes in the hamper, and Victoria had just given up. This was one of those times when you have to pick your battles, and this was one she was just going to avoid.

As Victoria began to pick up the clothes, her thoughts turned to her husband. He was a kind, loving, supportive man. She had always believed that they were in this together. That whatever they faced, they would be fine as long as they stood strong together. But over the past years, Kurt had pulled away. For reasons Victoria did not fully understand, Kurt was angry. His reactions toward Victoria drove her feelings of worthlessness deeper into the darkness. She felt alone that Kurt had left her side. He was no longer her supporter and protector. He now had taken up the role of her contender, a stormtrooper to her Skywalker, Gaston to her Beast, and Captain Hook to her Peter Pan.

Victoria gently covered Olivia and slowly walked toward the kitchen. She maintained a sense of silence as the night radiated reverence. Victoria thrived off reverence. She found it to be rejuvenating. It was not necessary for Victoria to turn on any lights, as nothing was there in the dark that was not there in the light.

Kurt's work took him away from home. They spent more of their marriage apart than together. Yet Victoria possessed the strong belief that being alone did not mean being lonely. She knew that with each step she took in the darkness, she did not take alone. Just as she knew the location of every rug, piece of furniture, and wall hanging in detail, she also was aware of the small items that may be out of place, such as a dog bone left by her two dogs or a slightly moved chair that many detour her path, all making it possible for her to easily stumble. Yet even with these unknown obstacles, she ventured forward with no fear.

As Victoria knew how to make her way safely through the dark, she had faith that Heavenly Father knew the path to guide her safely through this life. At times, she did not feel guided but understood that she was free to make mistakes, to follow the wrong path. But she knew how to return to the correct path, to repent for her misguided ventures and continue on with his help.

Without thinking as to her destination because of these thoughts swirling in her mind, Victoria soon found herself standing in front of the large sliding doors in her kitchen, leading out onto a large deck overlooking her garden. It had begun to snow, and the lawn and trees had already taken upon the appearance of white glitter. What a beautiful sight. Victoria stood motionless, admiring the magic of the night. She thought back on something she had once heard: No two snowflakes are ever alike. Was this really possible? But of course, she thought, *Who am I to question the ability of the creator of the earth and sky and all that grows and resides within its realm? If such magnificent detail can reside in the simplest of flowers, grains of wheat, and the colors that engulf the sky at sunset, surely, that detail is present within each snowflake.*

Victoria gently opened the sliding doors and stretched her hand out into the night to capture a snowflake upon her plaid nightshirt. She loved the snow and the silence that it brought as it elegantly covered the earth. As she pulled in her arm, she reached for the switch that illuminated a small light under the large oak kitchen cabinets.

Victoria stood in amazement as she admired the beauty and detail of each delicate flake. It was as if the angels had meticulously cut each one by one just as her granddaughters had done to the ones that now adorned her living room window.

As the flakes faded, Victoria once again opened the sliding door further, this time stepping out onto her garden deck. The glow of the cabinet light was no longer needed as the white sky illuminated the night. Victoria stood in amazement as if she was experiencing snow for the first time. She looked upward to allow the flakes to fall upon her face. A reverence could be felt as the earth was silenced. The peace that she believed she had lost because of the wonderings of her mind was once again restored. "All was calm. All was bright."

As Victoria stood barefooted in the snow, only warmth could be felt through her entire body. She knew that for only a brief moment, she was standing beside the Savior, basking in his ever-perfect creation. She had been led to this spot at this moment in time. She was being given the opportunity to refocus and find peace. Yet in time, as the cold began to become noticeable, Victoria returned to the safety and warmth of her home.

She retreated to the living room where she could continue to watch the snow fall through the large picture window. She removed an afghan from the back of a chair, wrapping herself with the blanket for additional warmth. She almost forgot. What time was it? Victoria looked at the clock. It was now 12:27 a.m. December 2 had arrived. The one-year anniversary of her breakdown was here, yet she felt no different. She feared the arrival of this day for weeks. But her fear was in vain. She was not about to lose all that she had worked so hard to obtain just because a date on a calendar had rolled over.

As Victoria rocked slowly in a chair next to the large window, she reflected on the past year. On December 1, just one year prior, Victoria's parents elected to host a large family Christmas party. The guest list included Chelsie, her five children, and their spouses. Victoria believed that this might be her last Christmas with both of her parents, and she was correct. She wished for a more intimate celebration, but despite her pleas as well as those made to Victoria's parents by Kurt, their request was denied.

Victoria's parents lacked the ability to comprehend the magnitude of difficulties that surround Victoria's extended family, mainly Chelsie. As the days grew closer, Victoria and Kurt elected not to attend. Victoria elected to spend the afternoon with old friends until many of the guests had left the party. This decision was met with criticism from her parents. "Just get over it. Move on. Put your dislikes aside for one day. Grow up. You possess such hate." These comments and the many that later followed emotionally crippled Victoria. It was similar to the comments made to her as a small child. "Grow up." What did that mean? Victoria was not confused by the hateful attitude of her parents yet was left confused as to their reason.

On December 1, Victoria arrived at her parents' home early to assist her mother with preparing for the event. Anger was reflected on her father's face, and his comments and tone of voice were expected by Victoria. In her father's eye, she had always been the least important of his children. This was not Victoria's opinion; it was told to her by her father. What surprised Victoria as she was in her parents' home was the negativity that was thrust upon her by her mother. The comments that her mother made caught Victoria off guard. Up to this point, never had her mother ever hurt her so deeply. As plans to meet her friends were still pending, it was Victoria's mother who made the final decision for Victoria to leave.

"Get out. Go. No one will miss you, and no, you cannot have a gift. You can have what everyone else does not want." Victoria, emotionally beaten down, exited her parents' home and, with tears in her eyes and a broken heart, pulled out of the driveway toward downtown. She was alone. Kurt had refused to attend to avoid the pending explosion that he believed would erupt.

As Victoria drove to meet her friends, she was forced to pull over as she could not see the road due to her tears. What had just happened? Was she doing the right thing to avoid the party? Maybe it would have been better had she not driven the two hours to her parent's house. She could be home with Kurt even though their relationship was stressed.

As Victoria wiped the tears and continued to the address provided by her friends, she soon found that the address led her to a homeless shelter. This can't be right. Victoria reached for her phone just as her friend appeared on the passenger side of her car. "Welcome to your special day," Her friend Maggie stated. "This is just what you need to counter all the hate I am sure you just experienced." Maggie was correct. She knew the problems that had arisen in her life.

For the next three hours serving lunch, folding laundry, and stocking shelves, it was just what Victoria needed. No matter how messed up her family was, at least she had a family. Gratitude for her life filled her heart. She said a silent prayer, thanking Heavenly Father for the opportunity to serve. For the first time in weeks, Victoria felt whole. She felt as if she had received strength and that, to some degree, what she believed was broken within her had been repaired. "When ye are in the service of your fellow being, ye are only in the service of your God" (Mosiah 2:17 Book of Mormon).

As their activities at the shelter came to an end, Victoria was confident that the partygoers would be saying their goodbyes.

Victoria returned to her parents' home, yet as she pulled alongside the curb in front of their home, she noticed that a number of cars still remained. Stress overcame her, yet she refused to be cheated any longer out of participating. She had been filled with a new sense of purpose and hope.

As she walked through the back door, she could hear laughter and music. The party was still in full swing. Victoria had not missed it; she was bound to participate, but as she stepped over the threshold, it was as if she was hit with an overpowering feeling of doom. It was so strong that it took her breath away. As the party resembled a festive atmosphere, the spirit that lingered within her parents' home was not pure. As she walked into the hallway, it was difficult to see. The lights were all on, yet darkness loomed.

She approached her mother wishing to share her events of the afternoon but was quickly met with, "We didn't even know you were gone. No one missed you."

As Victoria stood at her mother's side, absorbing the words that had cut into her very soul, her father came around the corner. "What are you doing here? Thought you left. Why did ya back? You don't need to be here. We're all havin' fun without ya."

Words such as these were common to hear from her father, yet they still added to the number of daggers she felt had been plunged into her soul. With no response other than the tears that Victoria tried so hard to suppress, she again headed to the back door and, within moments, was back in her car, crying uncontrollably once again. *Why am I here?* she thought. Victoria questioned why she had even attempted to participate in this holiday event.

As Victoria pulled away from the curb, the joy she had once filled her soul only moments before was gone. Something was dark and destructive in that home, and Victoria was concerned about the influence it would have on her four children. There was nothing left to do but head home.

When Victoria arrived home, she believed that she could pour out her heart to Kurt and that he would share her pain, yet it was not to be. Comments in regard to her stupidity in attending in the first place were the only support Victoria received. Where was her hero? The man who she believed would share her life, joy, and pain? He had slowly pulled away from her, and now he—when Victoria needed love and compassion the most—turned his back on her.

The next morning Victoria awoke early. She had concluded that she was alone. The communications she had received from her children and parents once she arrive home were all but supportive. Each one of them informed her of what they believed to be her fault. What was happening? Victoria was confused. Maybe she was in the wrong, but for what? What had she done? What had she been doing to make herself look so poorly in her family's eyes?

Maybe she was the failure that others commented that she was. Maybe she was not a person of value. Victoria began to believe that the time had come when she could no longer contribute positively to her family. Her family all made negative comments against her and why? Victoria needed time alone, time in which she could think and reevaluate the past few days, weeks, and months. To do so, Victoria drove to the next town which was twenty miles away to spend the day alone.

As Victoria strolled through the stores, admiring the Christmas decorations and doing a bit of Christmas shopping, her mind began to become less bogged down because of the criticism she had experienced. As she took herself to lunch at her favorite restaurant, her spirit began to feel refueled. She was a woman of worth. She knew it, but the peace was not to last.

Victoria's phone began to ring with calls from Kurt. Victoria did not want to answer the call as she did not wish to break the peace she was feeling. Soon, her daughters began to call. Wishing to not alarm her family, Victoria texted her daughter that she was shopping, was fine, and would be home later that evening. Victoria was determined to gain peace. She wished to forget about the day before, forget about the hate, the negativity, and—above all—the words, the horrid words.

As Victoria attempted to enjoy her lunch, her phone was flooded with messages from her husband and daughter. The comments made were, in Victoria's view, unkind. She was trying to escape the negativity, and the only way she could prevent it from coming through was to turn off her phone. After a few hours, believing that her family would move on with their daily activities, Victoria turned her phone on. In doing so, she was flooded with a great number of missed calls and text messages, again, many very angry and rude. It was not long before her phone rang. She could feel a sense of fear race over her. She answered. Little did she know that she was to receive the final blow. The voice on the other end came from one individual who she never believed would ever harm her—her daughter, her firstborn.

The hate, anger, and accusations that flowed from her voice were beyond Victoria's belief. Where did all of this come from? How long had all this hate and anger been stored up? The words *sick*, *worthless*, and *horrid* were all spoken on the call that Victoria was forced to disconnect. The phone continued to ring as her daughter tried again to contact Victoria. The peace that she had gained was gone. She left the store, leaving her cart of gifts unpurchased, and walked to her car. It was time for her to return home.

Victoria was overwhelmed with emotion. She was confused as to where to turn. Just as she pulled from the parking lot, she was alerted that she had received a new text message. As she elected to ignore it, another and then another came through. Fearful of what awaited her when she arrived home, she believed it was best to see what the text messages stated and from whom. Victoria pulled off to the side of the road to read the text messages; they were all from her daughter. Again, the same words that had resonated in the call were there in written form.

Victoria sat stunned. In a daze she pulled back onto the road and continued to drive home. Once again, her phone alerted her to a text. Looking down, she noticed it was not her daughter but the adult daughter of Chelsie, Hilary. Surprised to see that Hilary had sent a message, Victoria once again pulled her Jeep to the side of the road. It seemed as if Hilary was concerned for Victoria and was reaching out to her with compassion and love. Surprised and warmed by the message, Victoria quickly responded. Almost instantly, Hilary replied, yet to Victoria's surprise, Hilary's reply was nothing more than an opportunity for her to voice her hate for her step-grandmother. Victoria was confused, another stab in the heart. Victoria's strength had once again weakened.

As Victoria drove, she contemplated the messages she had received. She was not completely shocked by Hilary's message because of Hilary's past encounters with Victoria, but she was taken off guard by her daughter's. Victoria pulled her Jeep over one last time. She had to reread the words of her daughter's message. There had to have been something she missed. She believed she must have read it wrong.

As she began reading, she realized there was no second-guessing as to the meaning behind the message. It stated that Victoria was and had always been a burden to her family; she was not a good example; she was weak and sick in the head; and yes, she was worthless. What words, what horrid words. Victoria believed they had been written in the heat of anger, yet she also saw for the first time that they were feelings her daughter and family had wished to finally voice.

Victoria was numb and dazed. Those words, those horrid words. Why were they necessary? Why would anyone want to destroy another human in such a way? Did they not understand the damage the spoken and, in this case, written words can do? Where is their sense of compassion and love? Was there really so much disregard for their mother? Why? Why now? Was the gathering of that particular group of individuals the day before allowed for the opportunity for them to discuss Victoria in detail? And what of her parents? Did they make their disgust for their daughter known to the partygoers as their negative comments to Victoria were spoken for all to hear?

What had happened to cause such anger and disrespect toward Victoria? What had she done to offend them? Was she really a person who was so unnecessary? So disliked that members of her own family lashed out at her? And what were the comments about being sick in the head? Were they looking for justification for their comments against her? Was she really so different, standing out, and living life on her own terms? They were using her as a means of escaping responsibility for their own problems. Or did they feel burdened by her, wanting her to be and act as they desired, not accepting her for who she was?

Victoria had always imagined herself as an individual who resembled Humpty Dumpty, possessing a hard outer shell guarding her, holding her together emotionally, and keeping out the pain. Over the years, the shell had become thicker and heavier. It had become a burden for Victoria to carry. But unlike Humpty Dumpty who had all the king's men helping to put him together again, Victoria was alone; she had only herself. On a cold and dark winter road, Victoria's shell broke. With the word *worthless* and *burden* weighing heavily on her mind, Victoria turned her Jeep a sharp turn to the right and skidded off the road. The maneuver was on purpose, yet as the car came to a stop, she was safe and unharmed; nothing had gone wrong.

Victoria sat in her jeep and began crying hysterically. She was angry at those who she thought loved her. She was angry at her parents. As a matter of fact, she had developed a hate for them because of their actions against her. She was disgusted with her husband and her children for their senseless mockery of her emotions and needs. But most of all, she was angry with herself. How dare she act in such a way. Had she been successful and left this life, there would have been no morning and no sorrow for her departure, only disgust. And disgust is what she felt for herself at that very moment. Victoria shouted out a prayer to the Lord, "What is my purpose on this earth? What is my mission?"

Now a year later, Victoria was facing the memories she had tried to put behind her. She now was stronger than she had been in a long time. She had sought help; her shell was gone. She was emotionally naked, and it felt freeing. She was new, ready to begin again. Yes, some still disliked her, but she no longer cared. At least, this was what she was trying to do. She was trying to live for her betterment and not for the earthly approval of others. But how—surrounded by individuals who do not see her as the Lord sees her—she was able to maintain peace? She does not walk alone. Only the opinion of the Savior mattered. Yet the world still broke through, hammering her down and working to destroy any peace as to the person she was meant to be.

Many times, over the past year, she had been alone. Negativity had become the family's weapon of choice and the harm which it produced at times brought about evil. There was no question that Satan was joyful to witness her family torn to the brink of destruction.

Now one year later, the arrival of the Christmas season had been hindered as Victoria feared the memory of what had been. She believed the reason the pain was still so fresh was her family's inability to offer apologies. She had always believed that the words *I'm sorry* were powerful, freeing, and accepting of blame, a step toward repentance. Yet she knew that many individuals, as well as members of her family, view it as a sign of weakness. "I'm sorry for placing you in a situation that brought you pain." Those were the words that would have begun to heal Victoria, yet she knew that we could only have control over our own actions; we could not dictate the actions of others even if they will benefit them. "I'm sorry." Two simple words possess so much power. Two words that our Heavenly Father needs to hear from us.

As Victoria thought about the last time she heard those words from her family, she was unable to recall. She knew that she had expressed them to her mother and father when it was evident that they believed she had made waves at their party. Yet she also did not remember anyone at the party offering the same regret. Victoria began to consider that maybe that is why she had become the target of much of her children's anger. They saw her apologies to them over the years as an acknowledgment that she was at fault and that she was flawed. Yet are we not all flawed? No one is blameless. "For he who is without fault, let him cast the first stone" (John 8:7 KJV).

The following March, Victoria and Kurt took Olivia on a nine-day magical vacation to Walt Disney World. They had been planning it for months. Olivia was such a wonderful granddaughter. She had an enthusiasm and imagination similar to that of Victoria. As they arrived at the resort, all were overwhelmed with excitement concerning the adventure they were about to embark on. It was only a matter of a few short hours before Kurt received a phone call from their oldest son. He was given the difficult task of passing on the news that Clive, Victoria's father, had committed suicide

Upon hearing the words, Victoria sat motionless for a few moments; yet for her, it seemed like hours. She was trying to absorb the information. She knew this day was not far off as he had attempted the act many times in his lifetime. As she waited for her emotions to surface, the first thing she felt was relief. Relief that his suffering was over as he experienced depression most of his life. Then came the anger. *How dare he do this to his family? How dare he do this to her mother? Everyone had suffered at his hand. Now even in death, he reaches out to inflict final pain upon us.*

Victoria decided right then that she would not shed a tear for the man who had brought such destruction to her life. She had already shed enough tears because of his abuse toward her when he was alive. She refused to shed any on his death. For decades, their entire family had danced around the wants and needs of her father. They had done all they could to prevent this day from occurring, yet if he was so determined to carry out these actions, there was nothing anyone could do. It was Clive's choice. She only hoped that he had found on the other side what he believed he would whatever that may be.

Days before Victoria's departure, she had received inspiration that her father was going to leave this life on her first day in the park, yet no amount of concern or worry accompanied this revelation. She knew that she had been prepared for this event, that Heavenly Father was with her, and that the Holy Ghost was her comforter. Victoria decided to finish her vacation, so she put a smile on her face and crawled into bed next to her granddaughter. Nothing was going to destroy her time with Olivia, nothing.

As Victoria lay in bed, she tried to push the thoughts of her father's death out of her mind, yet she could not help but wonder what pushed him to make the final decision. Did he plan it out? What was he thinking during the last moments?

A flood of questions began to fill her mind, forcing Victoria to put up mental walls to not allow them to penetrate. Her father had been blessed with health his entire life yet could not endure the aches that come to a man of eighty-three. What tore him down was the depression that he refused to address for what was Victoria's entire life. Clive had been given the gift of a long life, and now he had thrown that gift away. Discarded it. Wasted it.

Once Olivia had fallen asleep, Victoria awoke Kurt and asked for a blessing. She knew that she could always rely on him for matters such as this. As Kurt laid his hands on Victoria's head, he stated, "I bless that you will have joy in knowing that your father's suffering is over. I bless that you will have joy in the days to come. I bless that you will find happiness and experience joy with your granddaughter as you are together with her in this magical place."

Victoria sat in amazement. What a blessing, simple yet so perfect and profound! *To have joy*, Victoria thought, *is that not what life is about? To have joy? Life is not a journey of hardships with moments of joy. Life is a journey of joy with moments of hardship.* As the days followed, Victoria opted to remain on vacation at the wish of her family, and she did have joy.

Now nine months later, Victoria still had not cried over the loss of Clive. She did not believe he deserved her tears. She had shed plenty while he was alive because of the physical and mental abuse he forced upon her. Now that he was gone, he was facing what he had created on earth. Victoria believed the pain was now his, and she would find peace concerning him at last.

As Victoria nestled more securely in the afghan, she could now see that the snow had become so deep that there was no longer a distinction between her yard and the road in front of her house. *How beautiful*, Victoria thought. The first snow of the year was so magical.

Victoria thought back on Christmases as a child. What a joy she experienced as her grandma and great-grandma would come each Christmas for a long visit. The love that her grandma brought was astounding. Their family needed that love, and Victoria needed the peace and comfort that she found in their arms. No one seemed to be able to love a child more than a grandparent.

Victoria reflected on her young sister who resembled her father's side of the family and her brother, the only boy, who would carry on the family name; both were extremely important to Clive. Yet when it came to Victoria, Clive often stated, "My first child is like a waffle. You should always throw the first one out." As this statement was repeated over and over, along with other negative and hateful comments concerning Victoria, she knew that she was of no value to him and had to accept the negativity that he offered her as his true feeling. Yet in the arms of her grandmother and great-grandmother—Clive's mother and grandmother—all of this was forgotten. Victoria knew love. She wanted to be a grandmother to her grandchildren as they were grandmothers to her.

Her memories once again disturbed her peace. Why must she be overcome with so much sorrow when there was so much good to absorb? To counteract the negativity that had once again overcome her, Victoria focused on the snow. She wished so desperately for silence, the silence and peace within her mind, yet was fearful it was not to come.

Victoria arose and wrapped the afghan around her shoulders and proceeded down the hall to her small office, a space in which she had gathered books, documents, and photographs. Victoria had been researching information and collecting documents pertaining to the civil rights movement.

During her research, she became focused on the lives of the women who had lived through the era of slavery to that of Dr. Martin Luther King. The millions of daughters, sisters, wives, mothers, and grandmothers who suffered yet rose from the ashes. They lived, loved, suffered, and sacrificed for their families while fighting to survive in the midst of a society that viewed them as lower-class citizens, undeserving of rights and liberties. They lived in fear for the life and safety of their children, understanding they possessed little power to protect them. They withstood the prejudice that society had thrust upon them, yet in the eyes of God, there was no difference in the value of any of his children. The more research Victoria delved into, the more anger and disgust she felt for the so-called good-standing Christians who carried such hate and destruction in their hearts for those who possessed a different outward appearance.

Victoria had always believed she had been born in the wrong generation. She wanted to have had the opportunity to have ridden the freedom buses, sat at the lunch counters, participated in the protests, and marched with Dr. King. These women, black and white, carried with them the ideals that Victoria held dear. They possessed bravery, bravery which is difficult for many people to understand. *Why does the world focus so much on differences?* Yet many times, Victoria could be heard saying, "How boring this world would be if we were all the same."

Surely these women, according to Victoria, easily understood and empathized with Mary. A woman who also understood hate and who feared for the life of her child. She understood how it felt to be forced to flee as a means of protecting him. There did not seem to be any boundaries—ethnic, cultural, or religious—that removed mothers from understanding the suffering, pain, and love that Mary possessed. *This connection has to have been part of the Heavenly Father's plan,* Victoria thought. The event of the birth of the Savior was further reaching than she had ever before considered.

As Victoria sat at her computer, she waited patiently for the screen saver of falling snow to appear. As it eliminated the dark room, she had no idea what she was looking for. It was second nature for her to spend hours working on a number of projects. She marveled at the technology at her fingertips, yet she understood that it had just as much power to do evil as it did to do good.

Victoria often journaled her innermost thoughts and believed tonight would be no different. Yet as she preceded to open her file titled "Personal journal," she glanced at the window on the opposite side of the room. It was as if the sky was a solid sheet of white. Victoria was delighted, for snow always increased her Christmas spirit. As she looked back at her computer, the thought came to her. *What was Christmas?* She knew why she celebrated Christmas. She knew by heart the meaning of Christmas—peace on earth and goodwill toward men. *But what was Christmas?* There had to be more. Victoria pondered her question again: *What was Christmas,* not *what is Christmas?* She said to herself, "What was Christmas?"

For a brief moment, the thoughts of the past year left her mind. What was Christmas? *Was* being the operative word. Victoria thought of the event that we celebrate. "I know it is far more than the birth of the Savior," Victoria whispered. "It was a bond, a bonding moment, a bonding moment between a mother and child."

Victoria opened her computer to Luke 2. She read, "And this shall be a sign unto you, ye shall find the babe wrapped in swaddling clothes and lying in a manger."

"Swaddling clothes," Victoria said. "Swaddling clothes." Victoria imagined Mary carefully selecting pieces of precious cloth for the arrival of the Son of God. How simple this fabric must have been, as Mary and Joseph had very little in the way of earthy goods. Before the Christ child entered this world, Mary already loved him deeply—the joy and anticipation of holding your child for the first time. The times when you cradle them in your arms and lightly kiss their soft warm head were the moments that cemented a mother and child, a bond that would carry through this life and into the next.

But what about Joseph? He had been given the blessing of physical responsibility of caregiver and protector. He loved him and for more than the child of God. He loved him as his own. Victoria knew it. She felt it. The reverence that came over her assured her that Joseph was selected as Jesus's earthly father. Now as Joseph held the Savior in his arms, he was prepared to sacrifice all for Jesus, including his own life.

What about God? Victoria thought. *What about the eternal connection which God the Father had with Jesus? How hard it was for him to let him come knowing the outcome, the ending of his mortal state?* "We will never know," Victoria said to herself. "There is no way we can ever understand what emotions God possessed." Tears began to run down Victoria's cheeks. She knew that "God so loved the world that he gave his only begotten son." This meant that he loved her. Without any reservations, she was his child. He was her father—her father. How joyous God must have been as Jesus entered this world, yet there had to have been sorrow as well. Was that what Christmas was? A bond, a bond between a mother and child, between an earthly father and child, a strengthening of a bond that existed between heaven and earth. Was it the knowledge of knowing that our Heavenly Father loves us in a way that is far deeper than we can ever comprehend? "A baby, the birth of a baby changes everything," Victoria whispered. The birth of this baby would change more than Mary and Joseph; it would change, and it did change the world.

Victoria reflected on the birth of her own four children. It seemed as if she had always had their spirits with her as if they had always been beside her as she grew. Were they meant to come to her to be her responsibility? Victoria remembered the fears she had after the birth of each child. She was worried that she was not good enough or prepared enough to be entrusted with a child of God.

Victoria turned back to her computer and pulled up a picture of Mary. She wondered if Mary had any indication as to what lay ahead for herself, Joseph, and her newborn son. As Victoria sat staring at her computer screen, she leaned forward and cradled her head in her hands as she placed her elbows on her computer desk. She focused on Mary's eyes. "What did you know?" Victoria whispered. "Christmas is far more than your son's birth. You knew what was to be in store, didn't you, Mary? You knew the joys and sorrows that were to come, didn't you? Angels walked with you, protected you, and comforted you your entire life. They had to have been there." Heavenly Father loved Mary too much to not have poured blessing from heaven upon her in immense proportion. Just then, as if out of the darkness, Victoria heard a small voice say, "But he loves you also."

For a moment, Victoria was unable to move. The power with which this message was delivered seemed to have paralyzed every inch of her being. Tears began to flow from Victoria's cheeks just as she heard the voice speak once again, "And he walks with you." Victoria had been reinforced in her knowledge that despite the billions of souls that fill the earth and heaven, her needs, her pain, and her desires were known by her Heavenly Father. She had been singled out for greatness just as Mary had. She had the pleasure of bringing forth and caring for four of his most precious spirits from heaven, ones who were chosen to come in the latter days to prepare the earth for his second coming. The magnitude of this responsibility overwhelmed her.

Victoria was always grateful that she had been born in this day and age, yet now for the first time that she can remember, she felt honored. She was granted a close connection with the gospel of Jesus Christ. Had she been honoring this close connection? Was she taking advantage of the opportunity to serve him and follow him as she should, or had she absorbed too much of earth and forsaken heaven?

I am surrounded by heaven, Victoria thought. She was older, and her body was slowing down, yet she had the energy needed to care for and enjoy her granddaughters. Victoria then remembered a line in her patriarchal blessing: "You will always be surrounded by children, "and she was surrounded by children. It was her connection to heaven.

Just then Victoria heard a small noise. She once again placed the afghan over her shoulders and headed down the hall to her bedroom. She wondered if Olivia had woken up, but upon entering the room, she witnessed the small body of this precious spirit still cuddled in the middle of the bed surrounded on each side by Victoria's two small dogs. What protectors they were, ensuring that she was safe.

Victoria again walked quietly to the kitchen. She intended to turn off the lights and then rejoin Olivia in bed. Once again, Victoria witnessed the falling snow through the sliding doors. She could see how it was weighing heavily on the branches of the pine tree that grew next to the deck. Victoria moved closer to the door and pressed her hand against the glass to feel the coolness outside. How blessed she was to have a warm home in which to reside. Her blessings were immense, yet she began to once again became overrun by memories. Victoria felt anguish that she was forced to relive the pain of the past. Despite her desire to suppress the negative thoughts and emotions, they found a way in which to seep through and darken the joy just as they had tonight. There was only one place for her to turn, and she knew it.

Victoria pulled out a kitchen chair and fell to her knees. "O Heavenly Father," she prayed, "free me from this pain." A flood of tears ran down her cheeks. She could taste the salty drops as they dripped from her top lip. "Please save me from the pain. Give me the strength to be who I was born to be. Even if others do not understand me, give me the courage to go forward and be happy. Do not let me live in despair or fear as to what people think or say about me. Let me be me. Help me to be me. Help me to love me!"

One year ago, on this day, Victoria was no longer able to endure the pain and negativity. She elected to run her car off the road. Everything in her life had come to a head. She grew up believing she was worthless, damaged, and undesirable. Now as she was forced to endure the comments and actions of her family, her protective shell crumbled. It was gone. She was now naked, naked emotionally. Thoughts that her family was better off without her took over her rational thinking. Victoria remembered the embarrassment she was forced to endure as she admitted to her actions. She did not want to be like her father. She refused to allow her life to go down the wasted path that he had elected to travel. Victoria was an educated, smart individual; she knew when to ask for help and where to seek it. Victoria learned quickly who she could turn to, who she could rely on, and who would support her. For it is easy to help someone when you feel sympathy for them, yet it is hard to help when you feel anger or guilt.

Victoria thought of the strength she had gained over the past year. For the first time in her life, she was the person, wife, mother, grandmother, daughter, sister, and friend she wished to be. She had been ridiculed and judged by others for not being the stereotype of a mother or grandmother who they believed she should be. Now she possessed the strength to see that not living up to this stereotype was their problem, not hers. They were going to have to change, not her. Victoria was free to act and love as she wished. But above all, she was free to brush off the judgment of others.

As Victoria continued to kneel on the cold kitchen tile, she slowly became engulfed by a dark feeling of confusion. It returned as quickly as it left earlier when she began to pray. Victoria knew that she had let it in and that it was thriving on the pain of her past. Maybe she was worthless. Maybe the real Victoria was not powerful enough to fight off the feeling of failure that lay in wait for her.

Victoria began to rock back and forth on her knees, she refused to allow the dark spirit to invade her mind. She knew Satan wanted her to remain in the darkness. Yet why was the word unworthy so prominent in her personal belief of herself? Victoria stopped rocking and lifted her head which had been resting in her cupped hands. What was she unworthy of?

"I am not unworthy." Victoria spoke out loud. "I am not unworthy." With each statement, Victoria's voice became louder and louder. "I am not unworthy!" Victoria once again rested her head in her hands. "I am not unworthy," she whispered. "O Heavenly Father, why do I feel this way? What do I need to do to be worthy? To walk beside you? Why? Why do I feel this way? Am I really of value? Please, please, help me."

As Victoria continued to remain huddled up on the kitchen chair, the darkness seemed to subside. A sense of peace filled the room. "You are a child, my child." These words that had entered Victoria's mind made her once again become motionless. "How can I be worthy of so much inspiration all in one night?" she whispered to herself. Then once again, as if the Savior was standing right there, Victoria heard the words. "Because you needed me."

An overwhelming sense of comfort, a comfort that she had not felt before yet was familiar, rested upon her. The darkness was gone, it was as if a glow—a warm glow—had filled the room. It lasted only for a brief moment but was so powerful that Victoria knew it was not of this world. It was a peace that only could surround the Savior.

For the first time in the entire evening, Victoria felt true calmness, the ability for her body to be at rest. It was then that she felt a small hand rest upon her back and then a small arm wrap around her neck. Victoria lifted her head and nestled Olivia in her arms. She arose from the kitchen floor and as Olivia rested her head on Victoria's shoulder. She took the afghan and wrapped it around the two of them.

"I want to show you something special," she whispered to Olivia. Victoria then walked to the sliding door, reached for the handle, and opened it slowly. The whirling snow immediately hit both of their faces. "Look," said Victoria. "Look at the snowflakes." She and Olivia stepped out onto the deck.

Victoria showed the delicate snowflakes to Olivia as they landed on the afghan. They both turned their faces skyward to feel the soft gentle flakes on their faces. As Victoria watched the flakes falling from the sky, she followed their journey to the earth. She thought what a pity that their beauty is now lost. Yet as she stepped out farther onto the deck, Victoria began to follow the journey of more and more snowflakes as they twirled effortlessly in the night sky and then came to rest gently on the ground.

Was the beauty of the snowflake truly lost? All of the flakes would eventually fall to the earth; all would lose their delicate design. Why was so much effort put into their design only to last a brief moment? "See how the snowflakes fall from the sky?" Victoria pointed out to Olivia. "They are so beautiful because they are created by God, and he makes everything wonderful, just like he made you." Victoria had answered her own question.

Victoria thought, *The beauty of the snowflake is not lost as it hits the earth. Its beauty will take the form of water which is needed for our survival.* "Look," Victoria said as she gathered up a handful of snow from the railing on the deck. "Look how beautiful the snow is."

Olivia reached her arm out from under the afghan to touch the snow. "It's cold," Olivia stated.

"Yes, cold, but beautiful," replied Victoria.

Victoria had learned so many lessons tonight. The birth of the Savior had a purpose far beyond our comprehension. The bond created between Mary and her baby Son had a purpose. The bond between Jesus and his earthly father Joseph had a purpose. And the bond between us and our Heavenly Father has a purpose. And the beauty of the snow had a purpose.

As Victoria stood in the snow, holding her precious granddaughter. She saw that she has a purpose as well. She knew that all the pain she had endured that night and for the last year, decade, or lifetime has made her into the individual she was now. Despite the negativity that may forever haunt her memory, she was not worthless. She was created by the Heavenly Father with grace and beauty. Even if others could not see it, it is there. She was and would always be of value, just as the snowflakes under her feet. They may have lost their luster, yet they were not worthless. Their value was priceless. Victoria was priceless.

As Olivia rested her head on Victoria's shoulder, she held her tight. "You are as wonderful as the snowflakes," she whispered to Olivia. "You are loved more than you will ever know."

"Love you, Grandma," a soft voice could be heard saying.

Tears once again filled Victoria's eyes.

"Why are you crying?" asked Olivia.

"Because for the first time in a long time, I know that I am loved," Victoria replied. She was loved by Olivia, about which she had never had any doubt. She was learning to love herself—a kind of love that was very important. But above all, she was loved by her Heavenly Father. She knew it without a doubt now. She knew that she was of value; even if she did not believe it to be true, Heavenly Father knew it was true.

We are like snowflakes, possessing an indescribable beauty, coming to earth. But as we become enmeshed in earthly life, we may lose our sense of beauty and feel trampled, unloved, and unworthy. But we are perfect in the sight of God.

ABOUT THE AUTHOR

Jackie Hirschi is a graduate of Utah State University where she earned a bachelor's degree in psychology and history. She and her husband are the parents of two daughters and two sons as well as nine grandchildren. Jackie possesses a great passion for adventure and travel. Yet her greatest joy is found within her family. Jackie and her husband Kim, reside in Preston, Idaho.